Stockings & Small Quilts

Block Quilt with Heart Applique   *Patricia Knoechel*

Table of Contents

Fabric 2

Tools 2

Sewing 3

Cutting Strips 4

Decorating Techniques 6

Rail Fence Stocking & Quilt 8

Diamond Stocking & Block Quilt 12

Four-Patch Stocking & Quilt 16

Pieced Lattice Stocking & Quilt 20

Postage Stamp Stocking & Quilt 26

Finishing Your Stocking 30

Finishing Your Quilt 35

Binding 38

First printing January, 1998

Published by Quilt in a Day®, Inc.
1955 Diamond St. San Marcos, CA 92069

©1997 by Judy Knoechel

ISBN 0-922705-96-8

Editor Eleanor Burns
Assistant Editor Robin Green
Art Director Merritt Voigtlander

1

Introduction

For as long as I can remember, designing and making Christmas stockings has been an important part of my preparations for the holidays. I've knitted some, cut others from felt, and quilted even more. For years I worked in children's homes, and a handmade stocking filled with little gifts was the best surprise I could think of for my kids on Christmas morning.

My funniest stocking making adventure was the time my sister, Eleanor Burns, came home for the holidays and announced we were going to make twelve stockings, one for every member of our family. Eleanor had just written *Country Christmas Sewing* and wanted to teach me how to sew the strip stocking. Just imagine Eleanor and me cutting all our strips from polyester fabric –with scissors! (Well, it *was* the 1970s.) Those tacky but illustrious stockings became an important part of my family's decorating tradition for many years.

The stockings in this book represent my current design ideas. When Eleanor decided we should write a book and share the patterns with you, she realized we would be missing out on a lot of fun if we didn't design some small quilts also. With help and inspiration from my other sister, Pat, we explored the possibilities and did a lot of sister bonding along the way too.

I hope our efforts will be rewarded, as you find your favorite stocking to sew and share with friends and family and make us a part of your Christmas traditions for many years to come.

Judy Knoechel

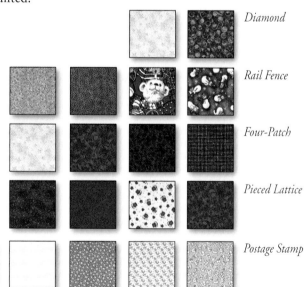

Tools

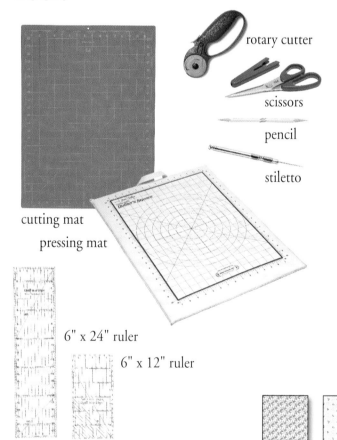

rotary cutter

scissors

pencil

stiletto

cutting mat

pressing mat

6" x 24" ruler

6" x 12" ruler

Fabric

For the stocking front and back, use 100% cotton fabrics in small and medium scale prints. The lining can be made from a less expensive plain muslin. Use thin 100% cotton batting, an 80/20 cotton polyester blend, or Thermolam, a 100% polyester batting. Fabric adheres to this batting, so it requires little pinning, and it does not lose its shape when machine quilted.

Diamond

Rail Fence

Four-Patch

Pieced Lattice

Postage Stamp

Sewing Suggestions

Use a fine, sharp, #80/12 needle. Use a neutral color thread such as white, beige, or gray. Use small stitches, approximately 15 per inch, or 2 on machines with stitch selections from 1 to 4. Use the same sewing machine throughout your project. Do not backstitch, except where indicated. Use 10 stitches per inch when sewing through batting.

¼" Seam Allowance

Use a consistent ¼" seam allowance throughout the construction of your project. If necessary, adjust the needle position, change the presser foot, or feed the fabric under the presser foot to achieve the ¼". Avoid using a generous ¼" seam allowance; this can reduce the size of your stocking base, making it difficult to fit the stocking pattern.

Assembly-line Sewing

Save time and thread when sewing several paired pieces by butting one after another without cutting the thread or removing from the machine. Use the stiletto to help push patches under the presser foot and hold your seams flat as you sew over them.

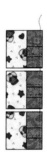

Pressing Strips

Lay the closed strip pair on the pressing mat with the darkest fabric on top, or as directed. Lightly press the length of the strip to set the seam. Lift the upper strip and press toward the fold. The seam will fall behind the darkest strip, or the strip originally on top. Make sure there are no folds at the seam line. Turn the strip over and check that the seam is pressed in the right direction.

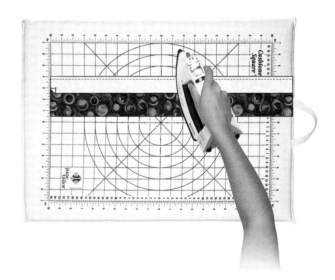

Cutting

Cutting Strips from Non-Directional Fabric

Use a large rotary cutter with a sharp blade and a 6" x 24" plexiglass ruler on a gridded cutting mat. Check that the measurements are the same on the ruler and the gridded cutting mat.

1. Make a nick on the selvage edge, and tear your fabric from selvage to selvage to put the fabric on the straight of the grain.

2. Fold the fabric in half, matching the torn straight edge thread to thread.

3. With the fold of the fabric at the top, line up the torn edge of fabric on the gridded cutting mat with the left edge extended slightly to the left of zero. Reverse this procedure if you are left-handed.

4. Line up the 6" x 24" ruler on zero. Spread the fingers of your left hand to hold the ruler firmly. With the rotary cutter in your right hand, begin cutting off the fabric on the mat. Put all your strength into the rotary cutter as you cut away from you, and trim the torn, ragged edge.

5. Accuracy is important. Lift and move the ruler until it lines up with the strip width on the grid and cut. Refer to your Yardage Chart for specific sizes.

6. Open the first strip to see if it is straight. Check periodically. Make a straightening tear when necessary.

Cutting Strips from Directional Fabric

For the wide second rail in the Rail Fence pattern, you may choose to use a directional fabric, in which the printed images are all oriented in the same direction. Cut one strip with horizontal images, and one strip with vertical images.

1. Open the directional fabric and fold in half, matching selvage edges. Lay the folded fabric on the gridded cutting mat, lining the bottom edge of the fold with a grid line.

2. Square the left end to straighten and remove the selvage.

3. Cut strip in designated width.

4. Refold fabric selvage to selvage. Lay on gridded cutting mat, lining fold with grid line. Square the left side to straighten. Cut strip to designated width.

Fussy Cutting Squares

A fussy cut is a fabric "picture" centered in the patch. A number of the patterns are perfect for this technique.

1. Cut a piece of template plastic to the required size.

2. Center the template on the fabric picture. If repeating same "picture," trace the outline onto template plastic with ball point pen. It will wash off for re-use. Cut around template with rotary cutter and ruler.

Listed are some sizes and quantities required for the various quilt and stocking designs. ───────

Stocking

Rail Fence	3½" x 5½" rectangles Cut 5 vertical and 5 horizontal.

Diamond	Cut (24) 3½" squares on point.
Pieced Lattice	Cut (22) 3½" squares on point.

Quilt

Rail Fence	3½" x 5½" rectangles Cut 6 vertical and 6 horizontal.

Diamond	Cut (12) 3½" squares.
Pieced Lattice	Cut (20) 3½" squares.

Decorating Techniques

Applique Using Paper Backed Fusible Web

"Picture fabrics" are readily available to applique to your project. With this method, pieces are flat, and edges are raw.
Applique before the patchwork is quilted.

1. Select the fabric picture for applique. Roughly cut around the shape. Place the fusible side of the web paper on the wrong side of the fabric to be appliqued. Make sure the fabric is larger than the paper.

2. Following manufacturer's directions, press the paper backed fusible to the fabric.

3. Cut out around the shape, and peel away the paper. Be careful to leave the thin web of fusing attached to the fabric.

4. Position the applique with fabric right side up. Press in place.

5. Stitch around the outside edge with a zig-zag or blanket stitch, using invisible or matching thread. (Depending on the thickness of the web, some manufacturers suggest a "no-sew" finish.)

Button Embellishment

1. Embellish your stockings or quilts with buttons, beads, or gold stars.

Applique Using Light to Medium Weight Non-Woven Fusible Interfacing

In this method of applique, raw edges are encased in the seams.
The embellishment can be stuffed with 100% cotton batting for added dimension.

1. Select a fabric picture appropriate for decoration.

2. Cut a piece of light to medium weight non-woven fusible interfacing 1" larger than the fabric picture.

3. Place the dotted, fusible side of the interfacing to the right side of the fabric picture. Pin.

4. From the fabric side, sew on the outline of the picture. Use 20 stitches per inch, the needle down position, and a clear applique foot if available. If the image is not clearly visible, trace outline with a fine point permanent pen.

5. Trim ⅛" away from the stitching.

6. Cut a small hole in the center of the interfacing. Turn right side out through the hole.

7. Optional: Cut the shape from 100% cotton batting, and insert through the hole.

8. Fuse or pin in place. Hand or machine stitch around the outside edge.

7

Rail Fence Stocking and Quilt

Stocking

Rail 1 and 3	¼ yd of each (2) 1½" strips of each
Rail 2 Nondirectional Or Rail 2 Directional	⅓ yd (2) 3½" strips ⅞ yd (enough for backing too) (2) 3½" strips (Cut one strip in each direction)
Batting	16" x 21"
Lining	½ yd
Backing	½ yd
Cuff & Hanger	⅓ yd

Finished Stocking Size:
Approximately 17" high

Quilt

Rail 1 and 3	¼ yd of each (2) 1½" strips of each
Rail 2 Nondirectional Or Rail 2 Directional	⅓ yd (2) 3½" strips ⅞ yd (enough for backing too) (2) 3½" strips (Cut one strip in each direction)
Folded Border	⅛ yd (2) 1¼" strips
First Border	¼ yd (2) 1½" strips
Second Border	⅓ yd (3) 3¼" strips
Batting	24" x 28"
Backing	⅝ yd
Binding	¼ yd (3) 2½" strips

Finished Quilt Size: 27" x 22"

Making the Blocks

Decide which strips are #1 and #3.

1. Stack and arrange the folded strips to the right of the sewing machine.

2. With right sides together, sew the length of the strips.

R1 R2 R3   R1 R2 R3

3. Set seams.

4. Press open.

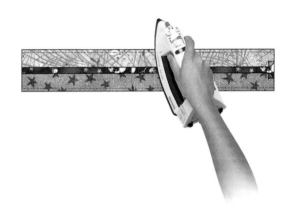

5. Lay strips on gridded cutting mat, lining bottom edge with grid line. Measure the width of strip in three places. Find best average, which will be approximately 5½".

6. Square left side to straighten and remove selvage.

7. Cut square blocks at your measurement.

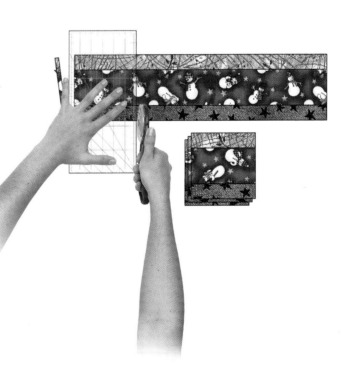

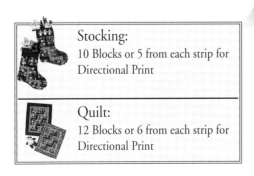

| Stocking: |
| 10 Blocks or 5 from each strip for Directional Print |

| Quilt: |
| 12 Blocks or 6 from each strip for Directional Print |

Sewing the Blocks Together

1. Arrange your blocks in layout.

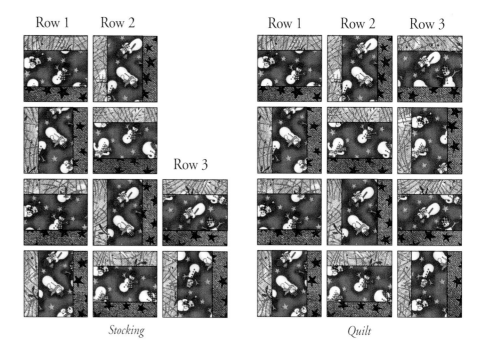

Stocking

Quilt

2. Flip blocks in vertical Row 2 right sides together with blocks in Row 1.

3. Stack pairs, keeping first blocks on top. Match outside edges as you assembly-line sew.

Rows 1 & 2

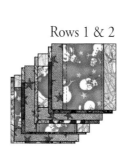

Row 3

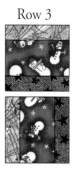

Stocking

4. Do not clip connecting threads.

5. Open blocks. Check to see if blocks are turned in pattern.

6. Add Row 3.

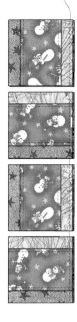

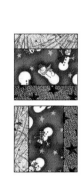

Stocking

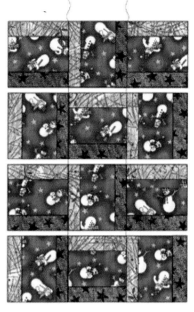

Quilt

7. Flip top row down onto next row. Pin and sew, pushing vertical seams in opposite direction every other block.

8. Sew additional rows.

9. Press.
   Stocking: Turn to page 30 for finishing instructions. Quilt: Turn to page 35 for finishing instructions.

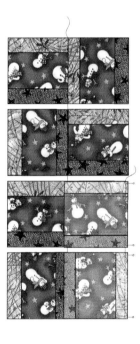

Six Block Rail Fence Quilt
by Patricia Knoechel

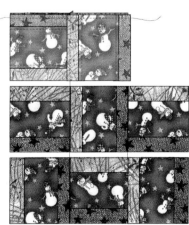

Diamond Stocking and Block Quilt

Stocking

Diamond	⅓ yd	
Or		(2) 3½" strips
Fussy Cuts on Point		(24) 3½" squares
Lattice	⅜ yd	
		(7) 1½" strips
Batting	16" x 21"	
Lining	½ yd	
Backing	½ yd	
Cuff & Hanger	⅓ yd	

Finished Stocking Size:
Approximately 17" high

Quilt

Block	⅓ yd	
Or		(2) 3½" strips
Fussy Cuts		(12) 3½" squares
Lattice	⅜ yd	
		(4) 1½" strips
Fussy Cuts Only		Cut one strip into (12) 3½" pieces
Batting	23" x 20"	
Backing	⅝ yd	
Folded Border	⅛ yd	
		(2) 1¼" strips
Border	¼ yd	
		(2) 2¼" strips
Binding	¼ yd	
		(2) 2½" strips

Finished
Quilt Size:
21" x 17"

Making the Blocks

1. Stack the folded strips to the right of the sewing machine.

2. With right sides together, sew the length of the strips.

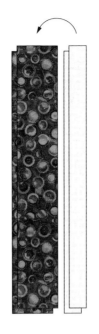

Stocking: Stack (24) Fussy Cut Squares or Appliqued Squares and (24) 3½" x 1½" Lattice Strips.

Quilt: Stack (12) Fussy Cut Squares or Appliqued Squares and (12) 3½" x 1½" Lattice Strips.

3. Lay closed strips on the pressing mat with lattice strip on top.

4. Set the seam and press open.

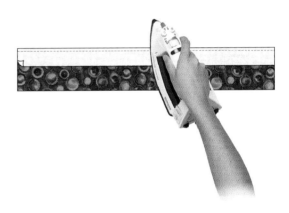

5. Sew strips together. Sew fussy cuts into pairs.

6. Lay closed strips on the pressing mat with lattice on top.

7. Set the seam and press open.

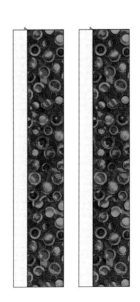

8. Lay sewn strips on gridded cutting mat, lining bottom edge with grid line. Square left side.

9. Cut 3½" wide blocks.

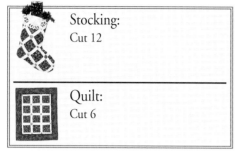

Stocking:	Cut 12
Quilt:	Cut 6

10. Divide blocks into stacks.

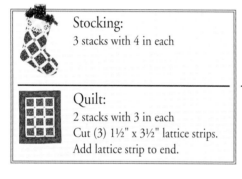

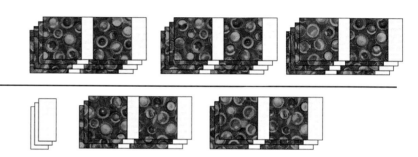

Stocking:	3 stacks with 4 in each
Quilt:	2 stacks with 3 in each Cut (3) 1½" x 3½" lattice strips. Add lattice strip to end.

11. Flip blocks right sides together. Sew. Clip connecting threads.

12. Press and direct seams under lattice.

Adding the Vertical Lattice

1. Lay stack of blocks and lattice strips to left of sewing machine. With block on top, sew right sides together with lattice strip.

2. Sew lattice strip to opposite side of last block.

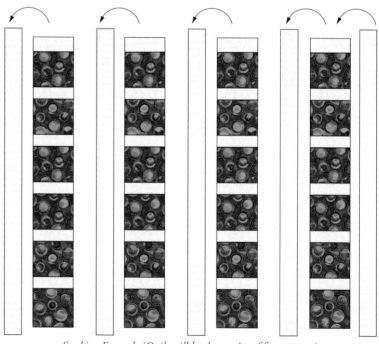

Stocking Example (Quilt will be three strips of four squares)

3. Lay sewn strips on gridded cutting mat with block side on top. Square, removing excess lattice at both ends.

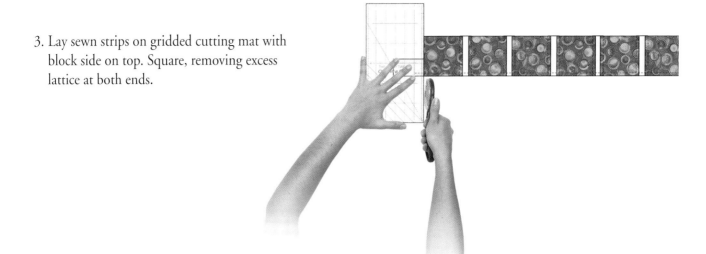

4. Lay closed strips on pressing mat with lattice on top. Set seam and press open.

5. Lay out strips.

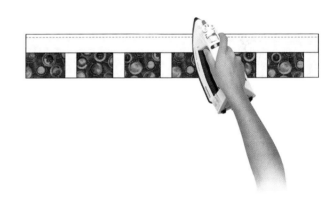

6. Line top edge of ruler with seam line on lattice. Back off ruler a pencil line width. Draw a pencil mark in the seam allowance.

7. Flip first row to second, right sides together.

8. Pin match pencil lines to lattice seams. Sew.

9. Repeat for remaining rows.

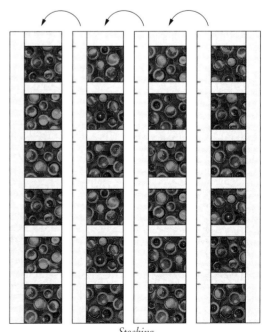

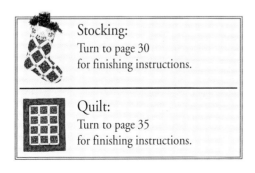

Stocking:
Turn to page 30
for finishing instructions.

Quilt:
Turn to page 35
for finishing instructions.

Stocking

Four-Patch Stocking and Quilt

Stocking

Four-Patch Light	¼ yd	
		(2) 2" strips
Four-Patch Dark	¼ yd	
		(2) 2" strips
Or		
Four-Patch Scraps		(8) 2" x 10½" strips
Lattice	⅓ yd	
		(6) 1½" strips
Batting	16" x 21"	
Lining	½ yd	
Backing	½ yd	
Cuff & Hanger	⅓ yd	

Finished Stocking Size:
Approximately 17" high

Quilt

Four-Patch Light	¼ yd	
		(2) 2" strips
Four-Patch Dark	¼ yd	
		(2) 2" strips
Or		
Four-Patch Scraps		(8) 2" x 10½" strips
Lattice	⅓ yd	(7) 1½" strips
Border	⅜ yd	(3) 2¼" strips
Backing	⅔ yd	
Batting	23" x 27"	
Binding	¼ yd	(3) 2½" strips

Finished Quilt Size: 21" x 25"

Making the Blocks

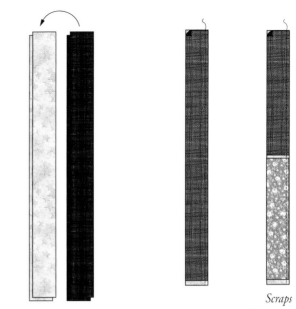

Scraps
Cut apart into
10½" sections.

1. Stack the strips to the right of the sewing machine.

2. With right sides together, sew the length of the strips. Butt 10½" scraps after each other.

3. Lay closed strips on the pressing mat with dark on top. Set the seams and press open.

4. Lay one set of strips on the pressing mat right side up. Place light across top. Lay a second strip set right sides together to it, with dark across the top.

5. Lightly press to lock the seams.

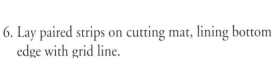

6. Lay paired strips on cutting mat, lining bottom edge with grid line.

7. Square left end to straighten and remove selvage.

8. Cut (20) 2" paired blocks.

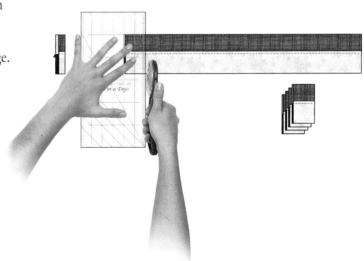

9. Assembly-line sew pairs together, matching ends and seams. Clip connecting threads.

10. Set the seam, and press open.

Adding Lattice Strips

1. Stack blocks right side down to left of sewing machine with dark square on top right.

2. Place a 1½" lattice strip right side up under presser foot. Assembly-line sew all blocks.

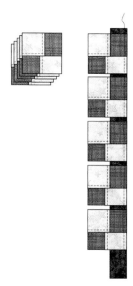

3. Cut apart between blocks. Sliver trim if necessary.

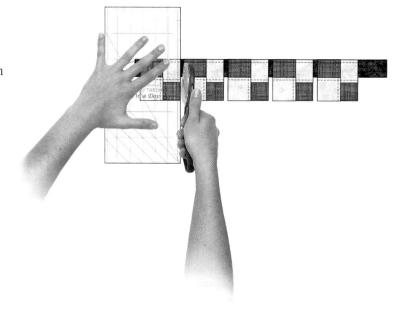

4. Stack on pressing mat with strip on top. Set seam. Open and press seam toward strip.

5. Make 5 stacks of four each. Mix up scrap blocks.

6. Assembly-line sew into four sets of five. Assembly-line sew a lattice strip to each end.

7. Press seams toward the lattice. Return to layout.

8. Lay out block strips with vertical lattice.

9. Sew together with blocks on top.

10. Trim ends, removing extra lattice. Return to layout.

11. Line up top edge of ruler with seam line on block. Back off ruler a pencil line width. Draw a pencil mark in the seam allowance.

12. **Sew rows together, matching pencil lines to lattice seams.**

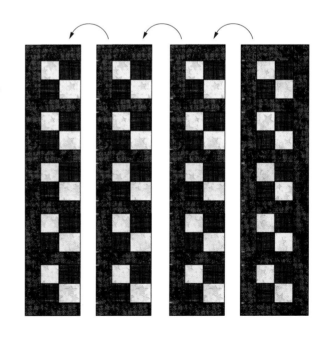

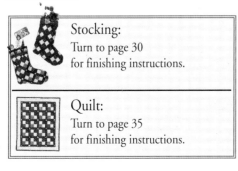

Stocking:
Turn to page 30
for finishing instructions.

Quilt:
Turn to page 35
for finishing instructions.

Pieced Lattice Stocking and Quilt

Stocking

Fabric A	¼ yd	
		(4) 1½" strips
Fabric B	¼ yd	
		(2) 1½" strips
Cornerstone (C)	⅛ yd	
		(1) 1½" strip
Square	⅓ yd	(Cut later)
Batting	16" x 21"	
Lining	½ yd	
Backing	½ yd	
Cuff & Hanger	⅓ yd	

Finished Stocking Size:
Approximately 17" high

Quilt

Fabric A	¼ yd	
		(5) 1½" strips
Fabric B	¼ yd	
		(3) 1½" strips
Cornerstone (C)	⅛ yd	
		(2) 1½" strips
Square	⅓ yd	(Cut later)
Batting	25" x 29"	
Backing	⅝ yd	
First Border	⅛ yd	
		(2) 1½" strips
Second Border	⅓ yd	
		(3) 3" strips
Binding	¼ yd	
		(3) 2½" strips

Finished Quilt Size: 23" x 27"

Making the Blocks

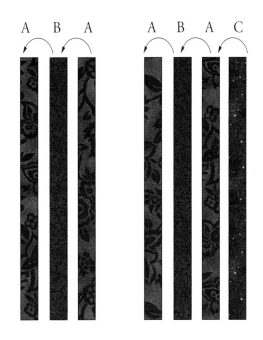

1. Arrange single strips in order to the right of the sewing machine. Set extras aside.

2. With right sides together, sew the length of the strips.

3. Set the seams, and press to one side. Set the A/B/A/C section aside.

4. Measure the width of the A/B/A section. Find the best average, approximately 3½". Record measurement.

5. Lay A/B/A section on gridded cutting mat, lining bottom edge with grid line. Square left side to remove selvage. Cut 1½" lattice strips. Stack seams in same direction.

Stocking: (22) 1½" lattice strips	
Quilt: (24) 1½" lattice strips	

6. Refer to measurement in Step 4. Cut two strips at that width selvage to selvage from Square fabric.

7. Lay paired strips on gridded cutting mat, lining bottom edge with grid line. Cut into squares.

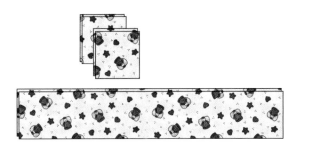

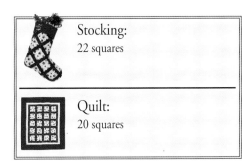

Stocking: 22 squares	
Quilt: 20 squares	

8. Lay out the 1½" lattice strips right side down with the seams facing down. Lay the Squares right side up.

Fussy cut for quilt   *Fussy cut for stocking*

9. Assembly-line sew lattice strips to Squares. Clip connecting threads. Stack with seams going in same direction.

10. Lay on pressing mat with Square on top. Press to set seam and open, pressing seam toward Square.

11. Assembly-line sew blocks together.

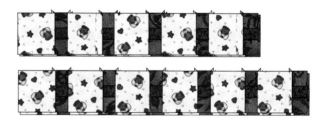

 Stocking:
Sew two sets of five blocks and two sets of six blocks.

 Quilt:
Sew four sets of five blocks. Add an A/B/A section to the end of each one.

12. Set seams and press behind Squares.

Cutting the Lattice and Cornerstone Strips

1. Fold the A/B/A/C section in half lengthwise. Use scissors and cut at fold.

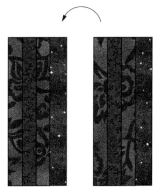

2. Flip two halves right sides together, and sew A strip to Cornerstone strip. Press seam to one side.

3. Lay on cutting mat. Square left end, and cut 1½" strips. Stack.

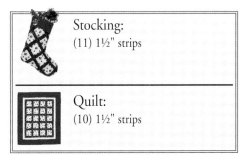

Stocking:
(11) 1½" strips

Quilt:
(10) 1½" strips

4. Assembly-line sew sets of strips together.

 Stocking:
Sew three sets of three together.
Two strips remain.

 Quilt:
Sew five sets of two together.

Cut remaining A/B/C strips in half. Arrange half strips in C/A/B/A/C order. Sew together and press seams to one side. Cut into (5) 1½″ sections.

Add onto other pieces.

C   A   B   A   C

5. Set seams and press under Cornerstone block.

6. Lay out lattice sections with Square sections.

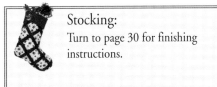

Stocking:
Turn to page 30 for finishing instructions.

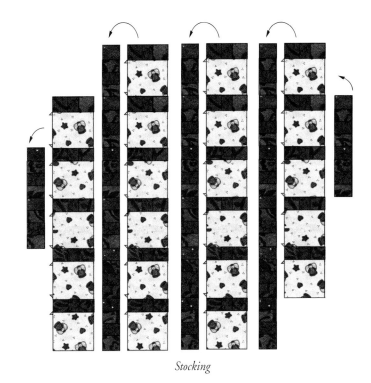

Stocking

7. Sew together with lattice on top. You may choose to pin at Cornerstones.

8. Set seams and press seam allowance under Squares.

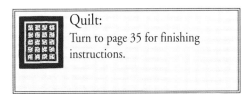

Quilt:
Turn to page 35 for finishing instructions.

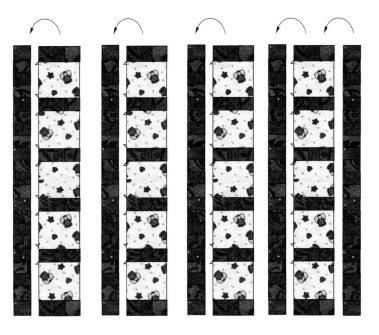

Quilt

Postage Stamp Stocking and Quilt

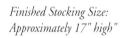

Stocking

Six Different Light to Dark Fabrics

	¼ yd of each
	(4) 1½" x 27" strips from each

Batting	16" x 21"
Lining	½ yd
Backing	½ yd
Cuff & Hanger	⅓ yd

Finished Stocking Size:
Approximately 17" high"

Quilt

Six Different Light to Dark Fabrics

	¼ yd of each
	(2) 1½" strips from each
	Cut each strip into 3 equal pieces

Batting	16" x 21"
Backing	⅝ yd
First Border	⅛ yd
	(2) 1¼" strips
Second Border	¼ yd
	(3) 2¼" strips
Binding	¼ yd
	(3) 2½" strips

Finished Quilt Size: 19" x 23"

Making the Blocks

1. Cut a 1" swatch from leftovers. Arrange in desired order and tape to a sheet of paper. Number 1 through 6.

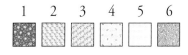

2. Arrange strips in order to the right of the sewing machine. With right sides together, sew strips into pairs.

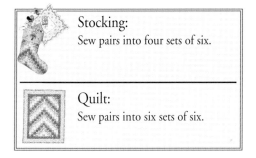

Stocking:
Sew pairs into four sets of six.

Quilt:
Sew pairs into six sets of six.

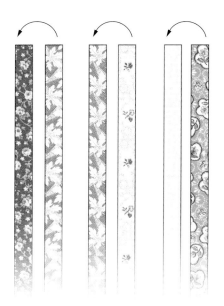

3. Sew sets of six together.

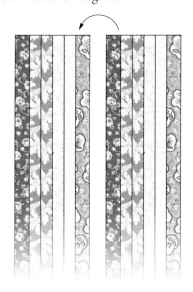

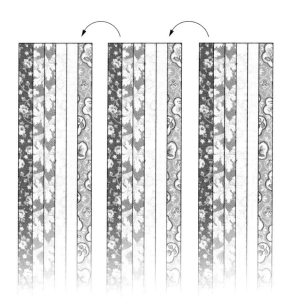

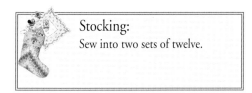

Stocking:
Sew into two sets of twelve.

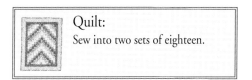

Quilt:
Sew into two sets of eighteen.

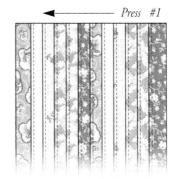

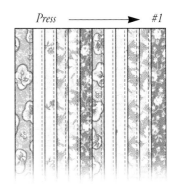

4. Lay one set right side down on pressing mat with one at top. Press seams away from one. Turn over and check for folds. Press right side.

5. Lay second set right down with one at top. Press seams toward one. Turn over and check for folds. Press right side.

6. Lay set on gridded cutting mat, lining bottom edge with grid line.

7. Square left side.

8. Cut 1½" wide strips from one set. Stack up. Cut 1½" wide strips from second set. Stack up. Do not combine stacks.

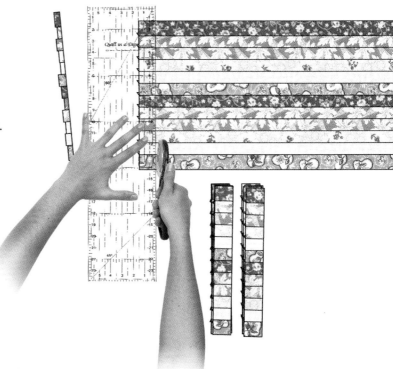

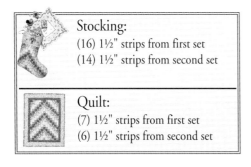

Stocking:
(16) 1½" strips from first set
(14) 1½" strips from second set

Quilt:
(7) 1½" strips from first set
(6) 1½" strips from second set

Stocking Only: Remove two strips from each stack for the toe.

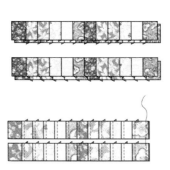

Sew one stack of strips into pairs. Sew remaining stack of strips into pairs.

Sewing the Strips Together

1. Start at center with odd numbered stack, arrange strips in layout, alternating between each stack. Double check that seams alternate up and down.

2. Sew together, fingerpinning to match seams. Follow specific instructions for each project.

3. Press right side. Press wrong side directing seams to one side. Check for folds.

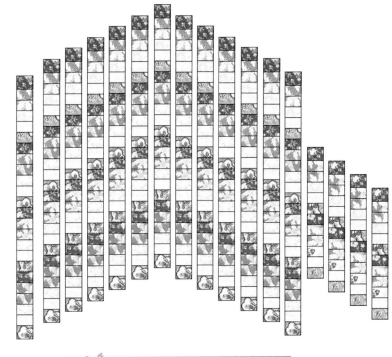

 Stocking:
Starting at center, sew together, moving down one square each time.

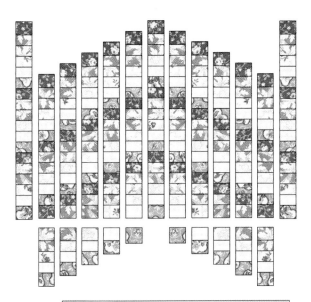

 Quilt:
Work from center out to sides. Unsew bottom sections as illustrated.

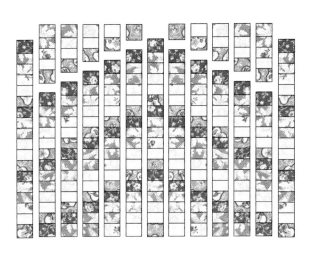

 Quilt:
Replace and sew sections to top of same strip. Repeat for all rows. Sew vertical rows.

Finishing Your Stocking

Cutting Out the Stocking

1. Press patchwork.

2. Lay out batting. Center patchwork on top of batting.

3. Pin stocking pattern to right side of patchwork. For Rail Fence and Postage Stamp, place stocking pattern straight on patchwork. For Diamond, Four-Patch, and Pieced Lattice, place stocking pattern diagonally across patchwork squares.

4. Cut out with scissors or rotary cutter.

5. Remove pattern. Decide where you will machine quilt. Pin stocking to batting away from quilting lines.

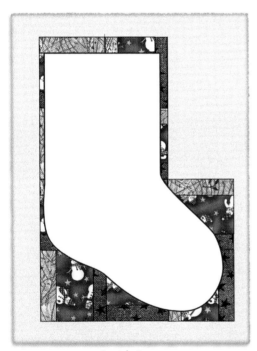

Straight Layout

Diagonal Layout

Quilting the Stocking

1. Place a walking foot attachment on your machine. Use invisible thread in the top of your machine and regular thread in the bobbin. Loosen the top tension, and lengthen your stitch to 8 - 10 stitches per inch, or a #3 or #4 setting.

2. Slide the stocking into the keyhole of the sewing machine.

3. Place the needle in the depth of the seam. Stitch forward following the design. Pivot with the needle in the fabric. Lock the beginning and ending of each quilting line with a ½" of tiny stitches.

4. Machine quilt on all lines, sewing the length or width or diagonal.

Completing the Stocking

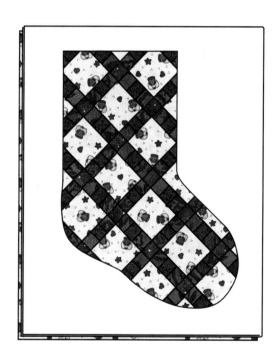

1. Lay out one backing piece **wrong side up**.

2. Lay muslin lining, folded in half, right sides together on top of backing.

3. Lay stocking on top. Pin.

4. Cut with scissors or rotary cutter.

5. Lay out quilted stocking, right side up. Lay the stocking back right side down on patchwork.

6. Lay both stockings cut from lining on top. Pin.

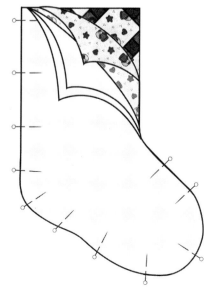

7. Stitch around the outside edge with a generous ¼" seam allowance. Leave top open. Clip at curves.

8. Reach between back of stocking and patchwork. Turn right side out. Check that all layers were sewn.

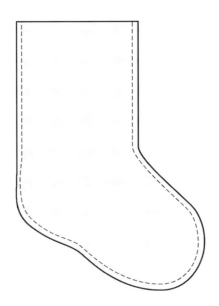

Making the Hanger

1. Cut 2" x 6" rectangle from cuff fabric.

2. With right side out, fold in half lengthwise and press.

3. Open and fold both edges to center crease. Press. Fold again. Press.

4. Sew ¼" in from fold lines.

Adding the Cuff

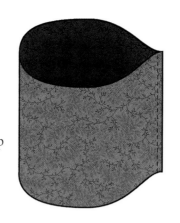

1. Lay stocking flat. Take straightening cut across top of stocking, evening up all layers.

2. Measure across the opening of the stocking top and multiply by two. Add ½" for seam allowance. Record measurement.

3. Cut cuff fabric into 8" strip. Cut 8" strip to recorded measurement.

4. Fold the strip in half, with right sides together. Sew the ends together. Press seam allowance open.

5. Turn right side out. Fold in half the other way to form a circle. The seam allowance is on the inside.

6. Pull two lining pieces apart. With the raw edges up and seam to the left, tuck the cuff inside the stocking between linings. Match the cuff seam with the stocking seam. Place one pin at the matched seam.

7. Loop the hanger. Tuck hanger between cuff and stocking to the right of the matched seam. Leave ends showing. Pin remaining edges.

8. Sew with a ¼" seam allowance around top.

9. Pull cuff out and fold down.

Facing for Linen or Doiley Cuff

1. Lay stocking flat. Measure across the opening of the stocking top and multiply by two. Add ½" for seam allowance. Record measurement.

2. Cut 4" strip at that length.

3. Fold the strip in half, lengthwise, with right sides together. Sew the ends together. Press seam allowance open.

4. Fold up raw edge on one side and stitch in place.

5. Cut linen or doiley about 4" wide and at least 8" long. A longer linen can wrap around to the back of the stocking.

6. Line up raw edge of linen with top edge of stocking. Pin through linen, stocking front and one lining. Using less than ¼" seam allowance, sew linen in place.

7. With wrong sides out, slip facing over stocking. Line up top raw edges.

8. Loop the hanger. Tuck hanger between cuff and stocking to the right of the matched seam. Leave ends showing. Pin remaining edges. Sew with a ¼" seam allowance around top.

9. Tuck facing inside. Turn stocking inside out and hand sew hemmed edge in place.

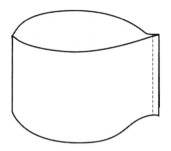

Finishing Your Quilt

Folded Border - Optional

A folded border can be sewn to the quilt top, or between two borders.

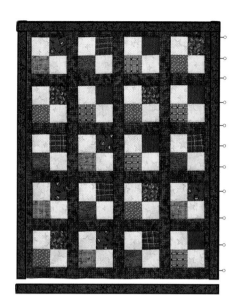

1. Press the 1¼" strips in half lengthwise, wrong sides together.

2. Measure the sides of wallhanging and cut two strips this measurement.

3. Sew to wallhanging, with raw edges meeting. Do not fold out. Use 8 stitches per inch and a seam two threads less than ¼".

4. Measure top and bottom and cut two strips this measurement. Sew to wallhanging. **Do not fold out!**

Sewing the Borders to the Quilt Top

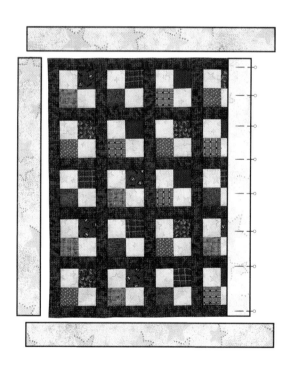

1. Measure down the center to find the length. Cut two side strips that measurement.

2. Right sides together, match and pin the center of the strips to the center of the sides. Pin at ends. Pin intermittently.

3. Sew with the border on top. Set and direct the seams, pressing toward the borders. Square the ends even with the top and bottom of the quilt.

4. Measure the width across the center including newly added borders. Cut two strips that measurement.

5. Pin and sew the border to the quilt top.

6. Set and direct the seams, pressing toward the borders. Square the ends even with the side borders.

Layering the Quilt Top

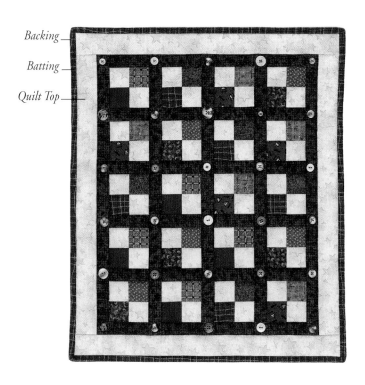

Backing —
Batting —
Quilt Top —

1. Stretch out the backing right side down on a table and tape down.

2. Place and smooth out thin batting on top. Lay the quilt top right side up and centered on top of the batting. Smooth and stretch layers until they are flat.

3. Place safety pins throughout the quilt away from the planned quilting lines. Begin pinning in the center and work to the outside, spacing them every 3".

4. Trim backing and batting to 2" on all sides.

Pinning the Quilt Top

Grasp the opened pin in your right hand and the pinning tool in your left hand. Push the pin through the three layers, and bring the tip of the pin back out. Catch the tip in the groove of the tool and allow point to extend far enough to push pin closed.

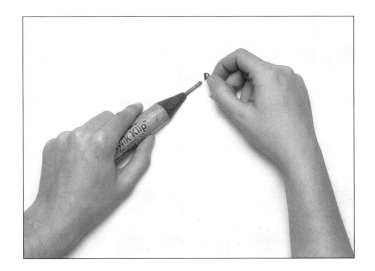

Quilting with a Walking Foot

1. Place a walking foot attachment on your machine.

2. Use invisible thread in the top of your machine and regular thread in the bobbin to match the backing. Loosen the top tension, and lengthen your stitch to 8 - 10 stitches per inch, or a #3 or #4 setting.

3. Slide the quilt into the keyhole of the sewing machine.

4. Place the needle in the depth of the seam and pull up the bobbin thread. Stitch forward following the design. Pivot with the needle in the fabric. Lock the beginning and ending of each quilting line by backstitching or using small stitches.

5. Machine quilt on all lines, sewing the length or width or diagonal of the quilt.

How to Achieve the Look of an Antique Quilt

The following instructions may be used to give your quilt or stocking an antiqued look. Use 100% white cotton flannel slightly larger than the quilt top in place of batting.

1. Pre-wash and machine dry the quilt top fabrics only. Do not pre-wash the flannel filler or backing fabric.

2. Once the quilt top is pieced, layer and pin to flannel and backing.

3. Using 10 stitches per inch, machine quilt the three layers together with quilting lines approximately 2" apart.

4. Machine wash on warm setting and dry at high temperature to shrink the flannel and backing. Put a large towel in the dryer with your quilt to prevent it from balling up.

5. Cut out and line stocking after washing. For a quilt, add binding to outside edge.

Binding

1. Square off the ends of each strip, trimming away the selvage edges. Seam the strips into one long piece. Clip the threads holding the strips together.

2. Press the binding strip in half lengthwise with wrong sides together.

3. Use a walking foot attachment and regular thread on top and in the bobbin to match the binding. Use 10 stitches per inch, or #3 setting.

4. Line up the raw edges of the folded binding with the raw edge of the quilt top at the middle of one side. Begin sewing 4" from the end of the binding.

5. At the corner, stop the stitching ¼" from the edge with the needle in the fabric. Raise the presser foot and turn the quilt to the next side. Put the foot back down.

6. Sew backwards ¼" to the edge of the binding, raise the foot, and pull the quilt forward slightly.

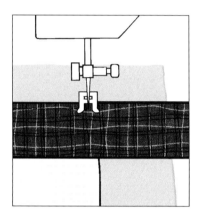

7. Fold the binding strip straight up on the diagonal. Fingerpress in the diagonal fold.

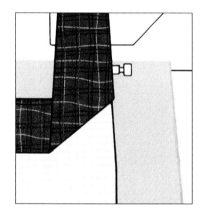

8. Fold the binding strip straight down with the diagonal fold underneath. Line up the top of the fold with the raw edge of the binding underneath. Begin sewing from the corner.

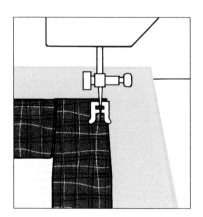

9. Continue sewing and mitering the corners around the outside of the quilt.

10. Stop sewing 4" from where the ends will overlap.

11. Line up the two ends of binding. Trim the excess with a ½" overlap.

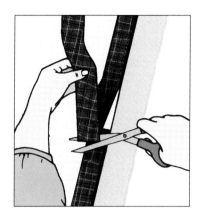

12. Open out the folded ends and pin right sides together. Sew a ¼" seam.

13. Continue to sew the binding in place.

14. Trim the batting and backing up to the raw edges of the binding.

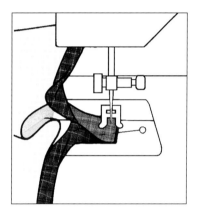

15. Fold the binding to the backside of the quilt. Pin in place so that the folded edge on the binding covers the stitching line. Tuck in the excess fabric at each miter on the diagonal.

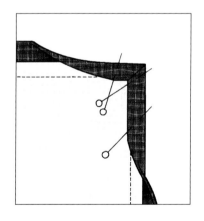

16. From the right side, "stitch in the ditch" using invisible thread on the right side, and a bobbin thread to match the binding on the back side.

   Optional: Slipstitch the binding in place by hand.

17. Sew an identification label on the backing.

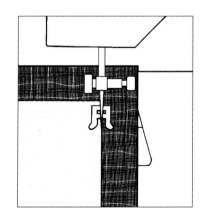

Order Information

Quilt in a Day books offer a wide range of techniques and are directed toward a variety of skill levels. If you do not have a quilt shop in your area, you may write or call for a complete catalog and current price list of all books and patterns published by Quilt in a Day®, Inc.

Easy

Make a Quilt in a Day Log Cabin
Irish Chain in a Day
Bits & Pieces Quilt
Trip Around the World Quilt
Heart's Delight Wallhanging
Scrap Quilt, Strips and Spider Webs
Rail Fence Quilt
Flying Geese Quilt
Star for all Seasons Placemats
Winning Hand Quilt
Courthouse Steps Quilt
From Blocks to Quilt
Nana's Garden Quilt

Applique

Applique in a Day
Dresden Plate Quilt
Sunbonnet Sue Visits Quilt in a Day
Recycled Treasures
Country Cottages and More
Creating with Color
Spools & Tools Wallhanging
Dutch Windmills Quilt

Intermediate

Trio of Treasured Quilts
Lover's Knot Quilt
Amish Quilt
May Basket Quilt
Morning Star Quilt
Friendship Quilt
Kaleidoscope Quilt
Machine Quilting Primer
Tulip Quilt
Star Log Cabin Quilt
Burgoyne Surrounded Quilt

Snowball Quilt
Tulip Table Runner
Jewel Box
Triple Irish Chain Quilts
Bears in the Woods

Holiday

Country Christmas
Bunnies & Blossoms
Patchwork Santa
Last Minute Gifts
Angel of Antiquity
Log Cabin Wreath Wallhanging
Log Cabin Christmas Tree Wallhanging
Country Flag
Lover's Knot Placemats
Stockings & Small Quilts

Sampler

The Sampler
Block Party Series 1, Quilter's Year
Block Party Series 2, Baskets & Flowers
Block Party Series 3, Quilters Almanac
Block Party Series 4, Christmas Traditions
Block Party Series 5, Pioneer Sampler
Block Party Series 6, Applique in a Day
Block Party Series 7, Stars Across America

Angle Piecing

Diamond Log Cabin Tablecloth or Treeskirt
Pineapple Quilt
Blazing Star Tablecloth
Schoolhouse Quilt
Radiant Star Quilt

Quilt in a Day®, Inc. • 1955 Diamond Street, • San Marcos, CA 92069
Toll Free: 1 800 777-4852 • Fax: (760) 591-4424
Internet: www.quilt-in-a-day.com • 8 am to 5 pm Pacific Time